GUIDE TO
CANADA

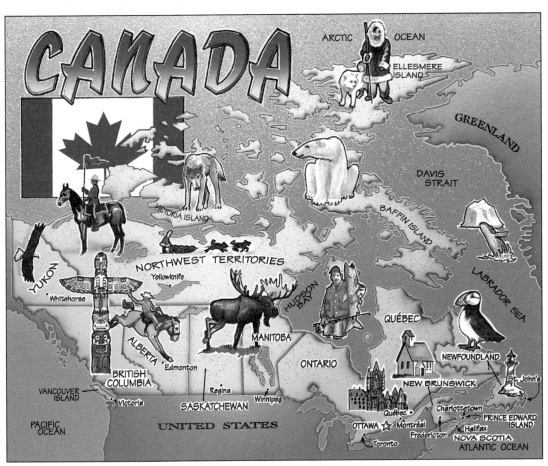

BRIAN WILLIAMS

Highlights for Children

CONTENTS

On the cover: Canoeing on Moraine Lake in the Rocky Mountains near Banff in the province of Alberta

Published by Highlights for Children
© 1996 Highlights for Children, Inc.
P.O. Box 18201
Columbus, Ohio 43218-0201

10 9 8 7 6 5 4 3 2 1
ISBN 0-87534-927-7

EUROPE

ASIA

AFRICA

AUSTRALIA

ANTARCTICA

△ **Canada's flag**
This became Canada's
national flag in 1965.
The maple leaf has
been a national
symbol of Canada
since the 1800s.

CANADA AT A GLANCE

Area 3,849,674 square miles
(9,970,610 square kilometers)
Population 28,537,000
Capital Ottawa, population of city
and surroundings 921,000
Other big cities Toronto
(3,893,000), Montreal (3,127,000),
Vancouver (1,603,000)
Highest mountain Mt. Logan,
19,525 feet (5,951 meters)
Longest river Mackenzie, 2,630
miles (4,240 kilometers)
Largest lake Lake Superior, 31,700
square miles (82,100 square
kilometers) — shared with the
United States
Official languages English and
French

▽ **Canadian stamps** English and
French words appear on all stamps.
These stamps show berries, airplanes,
the national flag, and the arts.

▽ **Canadian money** The currency
of Canada is the Canadian dollar.
These are the 5-dollar and
10-dollar bills.

CANADA

Legend:
- Ice
- Tundra
- Mountains
- Forest
- Farmland
- ★ Capital
- ● Major Cities
- ▲ Mountain Peaks
- — Country Boundaries

0 100 200 300 Miles
0 200 400 Kilometers

Provinces and Territories:
1 Yukon Territory
2 Northwest Territories
3 British Columbia
4 Alberta
5 Saskatchewan
6 Manitoba
7 Ontario
8 Québec
9 Newfoundland
10 Prince Edward Isl.
11 New Brunswick
12 Nova Scotia

ARCTIC OCEAN

Beaufort Sea

Greenland (Denmark)

Queen Elizabeth Islands

Ellesmere Island

Melville Island

Banks Island

Baffin Bay

Baffin Island

Davis Strait

Victoria Island

Cambridge Bay

Great Bear Lake

Mackenzie River

Inuvik

Foxe Basin

Pangnirtung

Yellowknife

Great Slave Lake

Dubawnt

Hudson Strait

Iqaluit

ATLANTIC OCEAN

Arctic Circle

Lake Athabasca

Ivujivik

Hudson

Arviat (Eskimo Point)

Churchill

Bay

Port Nelson

Nelson

Schefferville

Labrador

Edmonton

Jasper

Banff

Saskatoon

Calgary

Regina

Winnipegosis

Dauphin

Winnipeg

Lake Winnipeg

Severn

Albany

James Bay

Lake Mistassini

Gulf of Saint Lawrence

Newfoundland

St. John's

Prince Edward Isl.

Thunder Bay

Lake Nipigon

Lake Superior

Sudbury

Québec City

St. Lawrence River

Charlottetown

Moncton

Sydney

Montréal

Saint John

Halifax

UNITED STATES OF AMERICA

Lake Michigan

Lake Huron

Toronto

London

Windsor

Ottawa

Lake Ontario

Niagara Falls

Lake Erie

Ottawa

Rocky Mountains

© Oxford Cartographers

N
W   E
S

5

 # WELCOME TO CANADA

Canada is the world's second-largest country. Only Russia covers more land. Canada is a country of great natural beauty, with mighty mountains, lakes, plains, and forests.

If you arrive in Canada from its southern neighbor, the United States, you feel at home. One of Canada's two official languages is English, and you will see many familiar words and names on billboards. Yet Canada is different from the United States. It has its own traditions, and the people of each of its regions have strong feelings of local pride, too.

Canada is a little larger than the United States, but has a population only one-tenth as large. Most Canadians live in cities. About eight in every ten live and work within 200 miles of the U.S. border. Few people live in the rest of Canada, especially in the cold northern Arctic regions.

Canada has some of the world's most spectacular scenery. It includes parts of the Great Lakes and Niagara Falls, the vast prairie plains and forests, the northern Arctic tundra, and the Rocky Mountains. The people of Canada include people of British and French origin, and people whose ancestors came from other parts of Europe and from Asia. There are also smaller groups of native peoples, called First Nations. They include Indian tribes, such as the Dene, and the Inuit (who used to be called Eskimos).

The name Canada comes from a Huron nation word *kanata*, which means "to the village." Canada is a young country. Europeans first came here five hundred years ago. Canada was ruled by Britain until 1867. Since then it has been independent. Canada's mix of people, languages, and customs makes a land where there is much to see and enjoy.

▷ **Railroads carry people and goods across Canada** This train is passing the Yoho River in the mountains of British Columbia, in western Canada.

▷ **Vancouver harbor** This is the largest city in western Canada and the country's busiest port.

▽ **Objibwa native in traditional dress** Members of Canada's First Nations are proud of their cultures.

OTTAWA

Ottawa, in the province of Ontario, is Canada's capital city. The name Ottawa is from a Native American word meaning "buying and selling." It was chosen as the capital in 1858. Before then, Ottawa was not a city — it was a lumber camp on the banks of the Ottawa River.

The Parliament Buildings in Ottawa were constructed between 1860 and 1865. Today, they are the center of government.

The Peace Tower, built to honor Canadians who died in war, rises nearly 300 feet (91 meters) above the green-roofed buildings. It has 53 bells that ring out across the city.

In February you will find the people of Ottawa celebrating Winterlude. They make snow sculptures, skate, and also race horses and dogsleds on the ice. In summer you can watch red-coated soldiers changing guard on Parliament Hill.

▽ **Near Market Square in Ottawa** The city has quiet streets and small stores, but it is also an important tourist center.

▷ **Ottawa's Parliament Buildings** This is where Canada's government meets to discuss affairs of state. The city skyline is a wonderful sight, especially at night.

Canada combines a federal government like that of the U.S. with a cabinet system like that of the United Kingdom. But the head of the country's federal government in Ottawa is the prime minister, who is the leader of the political party in power.

In spring Ottawa has a Tulip Festival. The government of the Netherlands sends thousands of tulip bulbs every year as a gift to celebrate the friendship between the Dutch and Canadian peoples during World War II (1939-1945).

The elegant Château Laurier Hotel is one of the most famous hotels in Canada. Ottawa is also home to the National Art Gallery, museum, and arts center. Across the Ottawa River is the town of Hull, which is actually in the French-speaking province of Quebec, but is considered to be part of the capital city of Ottawa.

△ **Changing of the guard** The ceremony is held in front of the Parliament Buildings in Ottawa. The soldiers wear red uniforms and black bearskin hats.

TORONTO AND THE LAKES

Toronto, once known as Muddy York, is Canada's biggest city and the country's leading industrial center. This busy port city on the northern shore of Lake Ontario is home to "new" Canadians from many lands. All keep their own traditions, but as true Canadians. Every year the city holds a cultural carnival when they all have fun in their own style. Kensington Market is a good place to meet the local people as they go about their shopping. And Toronto's harbor front area is a great place to visit in the summer.

No visitor to Toronto can miss the tall CN Tower, which rises over 1,800 feet (548 meters) into the sky. From the top there are marvelous views of the city and of the ships on the St. Lawrence Seaway.

Drive about one and one-half hours from Toronto to Niagara Falls. The falls are one of North America's most popular tourist sights. The Canadian section of the falls is known as the Horseshoe Falls. Take a trip through the spray in the *Maid of the Mist*, the tour boat at the base of the falls — but be sure to wear the raincoat they lend you!

△ **Black Creek Pioneer Village** Here visitors can see life in Canada as it was in the 1840s and enjoy a wagon ride through the streets.

10

The province of Ontario includes a region known as the Golden Horseshoe because of its industrial wealth. In Ontario, you can visit Kingston, which was briefly the capital of Canada in the 1840s. Here there is a museum honoring Canada's first prime minister, John A. Macdonald (1815-1891). In the town of Stratford you can enjoy William Shakespeare's plays at the festival theater. You can visit the Hockey Hall of Fame in Toronto or go to the spectacular stadium called the SkyDome to watch the Blue Jays play baseball or the Raptors play basketball.

△ **Boats crowd the harbor in Toronto** Nearby are shops, restaurants, and parks. Above the city skyline soars the CN Tower, one of the world's most famous free-standing structures.

◁ **Niagara Falls** The Niagara River forms part of the border between the United States and Canada. The American Falls (on the left of the picture) are on the U.S. side. The Horseshoe Falls (on the right) are in Canada.

MONTREAL AND QUEBEC

Quebec is Canada's biggest province. In the 1500s French explorers came here, and today eight out of ten people in Quebec province have French ancestors. Some speak only French. Being mostly French makes Quebec different from all other regions of Canada.

The largest city in Quebec is Montreal, Canada's second-largest city. Montreal is the second-largest French-speaking city in the world, after Paris, France. Montreal has a subway, or *Métro*, and marvelous sports facilities in Olympic Park, built for the 1976 Summer Olympic Games. There are also fine plant gardens and an Insectarium with thousands of bugs! Universities include the famous McGill University, founded in 1821.

The capital of Quebec province is also named Quebec, but is often called Quebec City. The walled part of Quebec City looks more European than Canadian. This is the oldest walled city on the continent north of Mexico. The National Battlefield Park on the Plains of Abraham commemorates a famous battle in 1759, when British troops attacked Quebec City and took it from the French. The Citadel was built by the British in the 1800s, but most of the rest of the old city is French in style. As you walk down Rue St. Louis, with its cafés and restaurants, you might think you are in France. You can take a ride in a horse-drawn buggy to enjoy the sights. The Château Frontenac hotel is the most famous building in Quebec City.

Quebec City is a major trading center. Machinery, electrical goods, and other products from the province's factories leave Canada from the busy port here.

◁ **Sidewalk cafés in the old part of Montreal** Here you will find a great variety of fine restaurants, including French, Italian, Chinese, Indian, and Japanese.

▷ **Quebec City in winter** This nighttime scene shows the famous Château Frontenac hotel, built in the style of a French castle.

◁ **Place Jacques Cartier, Quebec**
A horse cab, or *calèche*, passes by. In the background is a statue of the famous English admiral Horatio Nelson.

THE SAINT LAWRENCE

Quebec City stands on the Saint Lawrence Seaway. This waterway connects the Great Lakes with the Atlantic Ocean. It is formed by the St. Lawrence River, several lakes, and a system of canals and locks. The Seaway reaches from Lake Superior to Montreal — about 2,400 miles (3,840 kilometers) — and serves other busy ports, such as Toronto, Hamilton, and Thunder Bay. Ships also call at ports in the United States, such as Buffalo, Cleveland, Detroit, and Chicago. Canada and the U.S. run the Seaway together.

To the north of the St. Lawrence is one of Canada's most important farming regions. The maple forests here provide the maple syrup that Canadians enjoy. Did you know that it takes 40 gallons of maple tree sap to make 1 gallon of maple syrup? Other foods from the region include blueberries, cheeses, and dried bean soup.

△ **Locks on the Soo Canals** Ships use these canals to pass between Lake Superior and Lake Huron. The canals are shared by the United States and Canada.

14

◁ A windmill and watermill
Reminders of Quebec's early industry still survive.

Forests cover more than half of Quebec province and produce lots of valuable paper. Quebec's mines produce iron ore and asbestos. Much of Canada's mineral wealth comes from the enormous horseshoe-shaped region known as the Canadian Shield, which curves around Hudson Bay and extends over almost half the country. The bay is named after the English explorer Henry Hudson, who sailed there in 1610. The world-famous Hudson's Bay Company began trading in furs in 1670.

Northwest of Montreal are the Laurentian Mountains. The rocks that form these mountains are among the oldest known, more than 600 million years old. The lakes and rivers of the Laurentians are popular with watersports fans.

In the east, where the St. Lawrence River flows into the sea, you can explore the windswept Gaspé Peninsula. This is where the French explorer Jacques Cartier and his men made their first landing in Canada in 1534. They were the first Europeans to sail up the St. Lawrence.

◁ The Gaspé Peninsula This region is famous for its hunting, fishing, and pretty scenery.

THE ATLANTIC COAST

The island of Newfoundland and the coast region of Labrador are the easternmost parts of Canada. Along this cold, harsh Atlantic Ocean coast, Europeans first landed in North America. The Vikings sailed here from Scandinavia more than 1,000 years ago. There are remains of a Viking settlement at L'Anse aux Meadows in Newfoundland. Later, fishermen from Britain and France came to catch cod in the rich fishing grounds of the Grand Banks. Today, fish stocks are low and cod is no longer caught. The soil is not good enough for much farming, but there are mines that produce about half of Canada's iron ore. Another industry is paper-milling, and offshore oilfields are being developed.

Newfoundland is a region of thousands of lakes and dense forests. Its rich wildlife includes bear, beaver, caribou, lynx, and moose. Thousands of gannets (white seabirds) nest on the ocean cliffs in the Cape St. Mary's nature reserve. People come to the Big Falls on the Humber River to watch salmon leaping upriver during their spawning, or egg-laying, migration. Signal Hill is famous as the place where the first transatlantic radio message was received in 1901.

Some people in Newfoundland speak in a mixture of old-fashioned and modern English. You may also hear folk songs that came originally from the British Isles, and the people of St. John's speak with an Irish accent.

The Labrador retriever, a popular breed of dog, was originally bred in Newfoundland. On the Labrador peninsula, some Inuit still trap and fish in the ways their ancestors did. Many other native Canadians have given up their traditional hunting way of life.

▷ **Signal Hill, Newfoundland** A battle was fought here between the French and English in 1762. Signal flags were raised to tell people that a ship had arrived in the harbor.

▷ **Moose in the spruce and pine forests of Newfoundland** Moose often wade into lakes to feed on water plants. A moose and the ducklike loon are pictured on Canadian coins.

▽ **Lighthouse on Cape Bonavista** The cape is on the eastern coast of the island of Newfoundland. This rocky coastline is very dangerous for ships.

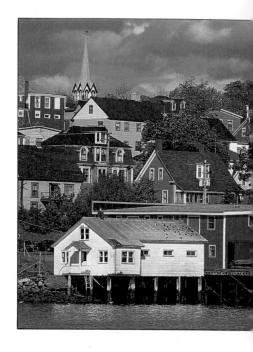

The three smallest Atlantic provinces of Canada are Nova Scotia, New Brunswick, and Prince Edward Island. The earliest inhabitants of Nova Scotia were the Micmacs, who lived by hunting and fishing. When the French settled here in the 1500s, they called the region Acadia. Later the British renamed it Nova Scotia, meaning New Scotland. Here, some people speak Gaelic, the old language of Scotland. Scottish music and dancing are part of local tradition. Another reminder of Scotland is heather that grows wild here.

The Bay of Fundy, between Nova Scotia and New Brunswick, has the world' s highest tides. At the head of the bay the tide can rise as much as 50 feet (15 meters). The current is then so strong that the Saint John River flows backward, at the Reversing Falls.

Halifax, Nova Scotia's capital, has one of the world's finest natural harbors. It is ice-free all year. The Halifax Citadel, a fort built in 1828, is one of Canada's favorite national historic parks.

New Brunswick's forests produce lumber and paper-pulp. The province also has rich reserves of minerals such as copper, lead, silver, and zinc. Most of its early settlers were people loyal to Britain, who came from America at the end of the Revolutionary War in 1783.

Prince Edward Island is Canada's smallest province. Charlottetown on Prince Edward Island is historic for the meeting that decided on the union of Canada in 1864. The island was also the home of Lucy Maude Montgomery, author of the classic children's book *Anne of Green Gables*. The islanders grow potatoes and also harvest shellfish.

▷ **Harvest time on Prince Edward Island** Farmers here grow barley and hay to feed dairy cattle. But potatoes are the island's most famous crop.

▽ **Lunenburg, Nova Scotia**
You can see the town church spire, houses, and painted wooden warehouses on the waterfront.

▽ **A soldier in the uniform of the 1750s** He stands guard at the Fortress of Louisbourg on Cape Breton Island, Nova Scotia.

THE PRAIRIES

Traveling west from Ontario, it is clear just how big Canada is. Four and one-half hours separate the Atlantic provinces of eastern Canada from the Pacific. Crossing the country was difficult before the Canadian Pacific Railroad was built in the late 1800s. Even now it takes four days to cross Canada by train. Prairie cities like Winnipeg began to grow only after the railroad arrived. Since the Trans-Canada Highway was built, cross-country car trips are possible.

More than three quarters of Canada's farmland lies in the three great Prairie Provinces. With their rich soils, Manitoba, Saskatchewan, and Alberta are Canada's grain-growing heartland. On these wide, open grasslands the farmers grow wheat, barley, oats, rapeseed, and rye. You will see fields of sunflowers, too. Tall grain elevators are often the only landmarks in the vast flat grain fields. Beef cattle are also raised, and most restaurants in this region offer steaks. Energy-producing natural resources, such as coal, gas, oil, and uranium are important to the area's economy.

The wind whistles across the prairies. The warm Chinook winds blow down the eastern slopes of the Rockies. In winter Chinooks are known as "snow eaters" because they can melt the snow so quickly.

The prairie cities have grown into busy urban centers. Calgary holds a famous rodeo called the Stampede. The city also has a stadium, built for the 1988 Winter Olympic Games, called the Saddledome. You can watch ice-hockey matches here. Edmonton has one of the world's largest shopping malls, with more than 800 stores.

◁ **Dinosaur Park, Alberta** Visitors to this national park wonder at the weird rock shapes. A guided trail leads to sites where dinosaur bones are preserved in the place where they were found.

◁ **A grain train crosses the Rockies** Here it passes near Jasper, a popular destination for visitors to Alberta.

▽ **The Calgary Stampede** A chuckwagon race thrills the spectators. The world's most famous rodeo is held every July in the city.

THE ROCKIES

Ride the railroad through the Rockies to get the best views of the mountains. As the train speeds west from Alberta into British Columbia, passengers get breathtaking glimpses of the scenery in some of Canada's national parks.

Tourists who stop here to explore this wilderness are in for a treat. It is great country for campers, hikers, climbers, skiers, and nature lovers. They can explore the wonders of Banff and Jasper Parks. These wilderness areas are easy to reach by driving along the Icefield Parkway.

Banff was made Canada's first national park in 1885. Ever since then its valleys, glaciers, lakes, and mountains have been protected for the enjoyment of all visitors. There are also hot springs, where bathers can swim in pools of naturally warm water. Jasper is the largest national park in the Rockies. In Wood Buffalo National Park, Canada's last big herd of wood bison roams wild. These bison nearly died out in the 1920s, but were saved. There are also wild beaver and muskrat. Canada's fur trade was based on these animals.

◁ **Lake Louise in the Canadian Rockies** On the shore behind the lake you can see the Château Lake Louise, an elegant hotel.

▷ **Banff National Park** This is Canada's oldest national park. There are hundreds of glaciers within its borders and several mountains over 10,000 feet (3,048 meters). The peak in the distance is Mt. Eisenhower, named after former U.S. President Dwight D. Eisenhower.

▷ **The resort town of Banff** Here there is a hotel built in the style of an old Scottish castle. Mt. Norquay looms above the city.

Some visitors enjoy fishing for trout and Rocky Mountain whitefish in the rivers and lakes. Others take peaceful canoe trips on Lake Louise, with flowers and pine trees providing a restful background. This is a great spot to try paddling a canoe.

The highest point on the railroad through the Canadian Rockies is Kicking Horse Pass, 5,339 feet (1,627 meters) above sea level. The pass was discovered in 1858 by an explorer named James Hector. His horse kicked him while they were crossing, and that is how the pass got its name.

CANADA'S NORTH

Fewer than 60,000 people live in the vast wilderness of Canada's Northwest Territories, although this area covers about one-third of the country. The climate is Arctic, and most of the ground is covered in snow in winter. The wildlife includes polar bears, musk ox, lemmings, and caribou.

Before the 1800s, the only people here were the Inuit and Dene natives, who lived by hunting and fishing. The discovery of minerals — first gold, and more recently zinc, lead, oil, and gas — has brought the modern world to Canada's northern wilderness. Some native people make fine art goods for sale. Others fish for whitefish, char, and lake trout in Great Slave Lake and in the sea around the Arctic Islands. Beginning in 1999, the Inuit will have their own self-governing territory, called Nunavut.

The city of Yellowknife, the capital of the Northwest Territories, stands on the shore of Great Slave Lake. The main waterway in this barren region is Canada's longest river, the Mackenzie. But the river is ice-bound for up to nine months a year. Travelers often have to use airplanes, sleds, or snowmobiles to get around.

In Canada's far northwest is the Yukon Territory. The country's highest peak, Mt. Logan, stands near the border between the Yukon and Alaska. In 1896 gold was discovered in the Klondike region, and thousands of prospectors rushed to the territory to seek their fortunes. Towns like Dawson City grew up almost overnight. Those wild days are over, but visitors to modern Dawson City can still try panning for gold. The largest city in the Yukon today is Whitehorse, capital of the territory.

▷ **A dogsled** This is a traditional way to travel and transport goods in the snowy Canadian north. The dogs can live in extreme cold.

▽ **A polar bear** Bears sometimes come into settlements looking for food. This bear was photographed near Churchill, Hudson Bay.

▽ **Forests south of the treeline provide valuable lumber** Mills process logs into wood pulp, paper, and timber for industry use.

BRITISH COLUMBIA

British Columbia is the third-largest of Canada's provinces. The largest city is Vancouver. Nearby Vancouver Island is the biggest Pacific island within North America. Victoria, British Columbia's capital, is said to be the most English city outside Great Britain, with its stately Parliament Buildings and elegant Empress Hotel.

▽ **Log cabins in winter** Away from the coast, with its warming ocean winds, winters in British Columbia can be very cold.

You can ride on sightseeing buses just like those in London, England. In Victoria you will also find a strange thatched cottage, a copy of Ann Hathaway's famous cottage in Shakespeare country, England.

Vancouver's natural setting among forests, mountains, and water is truly magnificent. A gun booms at nine o'clock each evening as a reminder of curfew time in the 1890s.

Vancouver's sights include the domed stadium built for Expo 86, Science World, and Gastown, where buildings of the 1880s have been restored. In Stanley Park you can watch sea creatures in the spectacular Aquarium. The Museum of Anthropology showcases fascinating artwork by the earliest people on the Pacific Coast.

British Columbia's many rivers provide hydroelectric power for industry and homes. There is mining for coal and minerals such as copper and zinc. About half the land is covered by forests, and lumbering is a major industry. Apples, cherries, and peaches grow well in Okanagan valleys.

Salmon swim up the rivers to breed, and salmon fishing is a vital industry. The rivers also provide sport. For a thrill, you can try whitewater rafting on the Fraser or Columbia Rivers, shooting through Hell's Gate or the Devil's Cauldron. Or, if you prefer snow sports, Whistler Mountain is one of Canada's most popular ski resorts.

▷ Totem poles Some of the finest examples of totem poles made by the native peoples of the northwest coast can be admired in Victoria's Thunderbird Park.

▽ Robson Square in downtown Vancouver In British Columbia's biggest city, people enjoy dining in fine restaurants and visiting theaters and art galleries.

CANADA FACTS AND FIGURES

People

Most Canadians are descendants of settlers from Europe. There are also about 50,000 Inuit and about 780,000 North American Indians. Most Canadians speak English. There is a large French-speaking minority. Because of successive waves of immigration over the years, Canada has a diverse population, including people from Europe and most recently from Asia and the Caribbean.

Trade and Industry

Tourism, manufacturing, mining, and forestry are important to Canada's economy. More than 60 percent of Canadian workers are employed in stores, banks, schools, and recreation services.

Canada has enormous mineral resources. It produces coal, gold, copper, iron ore, nickel, zinc, lead, potash, aluminum, and uranium. There are also huge oil and gas reserves.

Factories produce a variety of products, such as machinery, vehicles, chemicals, paper, and steel. A large part of of Canada's electricity comes from hydroelectric plants.

△ **A snowmobile** This is a good way to travel across the vast snowfields of the Athabasca Glacier in the Rocky Mountains.

Farming

Canada's main farm products are wheat, beef cattle, milk, and hogs. Three quarters of its farmland is in the enormous Prairie Provinces. Saskatchewan grows more wheat than any other province. Alberta leads in beef cattle. Prairie farms are very large, and groups of farmers work in teams to harvest the wheat and other grain crops.

Elsewhere in Canada, farming is more varied. Southern Ontario farmers grow vegetables and fruits, and British Columbia is famous for delicious apples. Another important farming region is the St. Lawrence Lowlands, where farmers grow mixed crops and raise beef and dairy cattle. Farms in the smaller Atlantic Provinces produce potatoes, grain, and dairy products.

Fishing

This is Canada's oldest industry, but the Grand Banks off Newfoundland no longer attract fishing boats as they did in the 1500s when Europeans first began to settle in North America. The most important seafoods are lobster, crab, and scallops. The Pacific coast fisheries concentrate on salmon, caught at the mouths of rivers, but also catch ocean fish such as bluefin tuna. Lake and river fish include trout and perch.

Food

Beef is a favorite with many Canadians. Other meats such as chicken and pork, as well as fish, are also popular. Carrots, beans, and salad vegetables accompany many dishes, along with potatoes. Canadians enjoy desserts such as apple, blueberry, and peach pies, as well as ice cream.

Each region of Canada has its own food specialities—shellfish in Newfoundland, salmon on the Pacific coast, and cheeses in Ontario, where ethnic foods are also widely available. Quebec is well known for its authentic French-style cooking.

Traditional dishes may include:
baked apple dumplings from Nova Scotia
flipper pie: fish pie from Newfoundland
tourtière: French-Canadian meat pie from Quebec

Schools

Each province and territory has its own school system. Most children go to free public schools, and school systems in most provinces have 12 grades. In some provinces, there are separate schools for Protestants and Roman Catholics.

University education is paid for mainly by the government. Some of Quebec's universities hold classes in French and English, others only in French. Most universities outside Quebec teach in English. Both languages are used for teaching at the University of Ottawa in Ontario.

△ **Wheatfields on the prairies of Alberta**
Canada is one of the world's leading grain producers. Wheat is the major crop grown on the prairies.

The Media

Canada has about 120 daily newspapers and more than 1,000 weekly papers. Leading English-language newspapers include the Montreal *Gazette* and the Toronto *Star* and *Globe and Mail. La Presse* of Montreal is the biggest-selling paper published in French.

Television programs in French and English are broadcast by the Canadian Broadcasting Company (CBC), which receives government money, and by CTV, a privately owned organization. Programs are beamed by satellite to reach even the most remote regions of Canada. There are also smaller independent, regional, and provincial networks. Many Canadians receive U.S. channels by means of cable links. CBC broadcasts radio nationwide, and there are many private radio stations.

Art and Drama

In colonial times, Canadian artists and writers usually followed European styles. Today, Canadian painters, sculptors, poets, and novelists are developing Native American styles.

Traditional artforms include the wood carvings of the Haida and Kwakiutl peoples of the Pacific coast and the stone carvings of people and animals made by Inuit artists.

Painters in the 1800s showed scenes of pioneer and farm life, as in the paintings by Cornelius Krieghoff. Modern artists produce paintings of landscapes and more abstract images.

Canada's best-known drama events are the Shaw festival and the annual Stratford festival, both in Ontario.

CANADA FACTS AND FIGURES

Literature and Music
Canadian authors have written in both French and English. Leading Canadian writers in English include Lucy Maude Montgomery, Stephen Leacock, Margaret Atwood, and Robertson Davies. Important French-Canadian writers include Octave Crémazie, Louis Hémon, and Gabrielle Roy.

Folk music is important in Canada. The country's musicians and dancers are famous worldwide. Well-known performers include pianist Glenn Gould, opera star Jon Vickers, and singers Joni Mitchell, Bryan Adams, and Ben Heppner.

Sports
Hockey is the most popular sport in Canada, with major teams playing in the National Hockey League. Canadians also play soccer, rugby, and professional gridiron football. The rules of Canadian football are slightly different from those of American football, and the field is bigger. Baseball and basketball are popular, too. The sport of lacrosse is based on a game played by tribes of the First Nations, who called it baggataway.

△ **Royal Canadian Mounted Police display at the Calgary Stampede**
The "Mounties" were formed in 1873.

Religion
Most Canadians are Christians. Roman Catholics are the largest group, with about 11 million members. There are several Protestant denominations. Because of its multicultural make-up, Canada also has many Jews, Muslims, Hindus, Buddhists, and Sikhs.

Festivals and Holidays
Canada has a number of national and regional holidays.
January 1 **New Year's Day**
Monday before May 25 **Victoria Day** Commemorates Queen Victoria's birthday

Second Monday in October **Thanksgiving Day** This is celebrated much as in the United States.
July 1 **Canada Day**, formerly Dominion Day, celebrating the founding of Canada in 1867
November 11 **Remembrance Day** In honor of Canada's dead of World War I and II
December 25 **Christmas**
December 26 **Boxing Day**

Plants
Canada's most famous tree is the maple, but many other trees, evergreen and deciduous, grow in the forests. The prairies are natural grasslands. On the cold tundra plains only lichens, mosses, and grasslike sedges grow.

Animals
Canada has a rich wildlife. The national animal is the beaver.

Large animals of the mountains and forests include moose, caribou, black and grizzly bears, wolf, wolverine, fox, cougar, bobcat, muskrat, and mountain goat. In the Arctic regions live musk ox, polar bear, walrus, and seal. Fish are plentiful in rivers and lakes and in the oceans.

HISTORY

The first people came to Canada from Asia more than 30,000 years ago. These people were the ancestors of today's Inuit and Native Americans. Europeans began to explore Canada's eastern coast in the late 1400s.

The Europeans founded Canada's first cities. They traded for furs with the native peoples. Wars between France and Britain spilled over into North America, including Canada. Britain eventually took control of the region, but French influence and culture remained strong.

Two British colonies, Upper and Lower Canada, were joined in 1841. Explorers and settlers moved across the plains and mountains. The North West Mounted Police brought law and order to the frontier regions.

The Dominion of Canada was created in 1867, forming one single country with its own government. During the late 1800s and early 1900s, immigrants arrived from Europe.

In 1931 Canada adopted its present system of government as an independent nation. The last province to join the federation was Newfoundland in 1949. Canada took a leading part in both World War I (1914-1918) and World War II (1939-1945) as an ally of Britain and the United States. In 1967, Expo 67 exhibition celebrated 100 years of Confederation.

Quebec separatists have campaigned for a breakaway from the rest of Canada. Separatists believe that French Canada has its own unique identity and therefore should be a separate nation.

LANGUAGE

English is spoken throughout most of Canada, but there are regional variations, or dialects. In general, Canadian English is written much like British English. *Center* is written as *centre*, and *labor* as *labour*, and *practicing* as *practising*. People use Irish and Scottish words and phrases in the Atlantic Provinces, especially Newfoundland.

In Quebec, French is often the only language used on traffic signs, store signs, and billboards. French-speakers of Quebec call themselves *Québécois*.

Useful words and phrases

Canadian	English
Bannock	Warm grilled bread
Bluenoser	Nova Scotian
Bombardier	Skimobile
Chesterfield	Sofa
Chinook	Warm southwest wind
Fiddlehead	Fern frond
Macintosh	Apple
Mountie	Officer of the Royal Canadian Mounted Police
Mukluks	Sealskin boots
Muskeg	Swamp
Serviette	Napkin

Useful words and phrases

Canadian	English
Skidoo	Snowmobile
Toque	Wool hat

Many Québécois use words with an English, rather than a French, meaning. For example:

English:	to marry
Québécois:	marier
French:	épouser
English:	change (money)
Québécois:	change
French:	monnaie

Outside Quebec, many French-speaking Canadians use English words mixed with French.

INDEX

Acknowledgments
Book created for Highlights for Children, Inc. by Bender Richardson White.
Editors: Peter MacDonald and Lionel Bender
Designer: Malcolm Smythe
Art Editor: Ben White
Editorial Assistant: Madeleine Samuel
Picture Researcher: Annabel Ossel
Production: Kim Richardson

Maps produced by Oxford Cartographers, England.
Banknotes from Thomas Cook Currency Services.
Stamps from Stanley Gibbons.

Editorial Consultant: Andrew Gutelle
Guide to Canada is approved by Dr. Gil Winstanley, Ottawa, Canada
Canada Consultant: Dr. Ronald Jobe, University of British Columbia, Vancouver, Canada
Managing Editor, Highlights New Products: Margie Hayes Richmond

Picture credits
EU = Eye Ubiquitous, JD = James Davis Travel Photography. Z = Zefa. t = top, b = bottom, l = left, r = right.
Cover: Z. Pages 6-7: Z. 7t: Z/Damm. 7b: EU/L. Fordyce. 8l: Z. 8-9: Z. 9: EU/JD. 10l: EU/JD. 10-11: Z. 11t: Z. 12b: Z/Kitchin. 13t: Z/K. Goebel. 13b: Z. 14l: EU/L. Fordyce. 14-15, 15t: Z. 16-17 Z/E. Weber. 17t: EU/L. Johnstone. 17b, 18t: Z. 18b: Z/Damm. 19: EU/JD. 20: Z. 21t: EU/J. Winkley. 21b: Robert Harding Picture Library. 22: EU/JD. 23t: Z/Smith. 23b: Z/Damm. 24-25: Z/Dr. Hans Kramarz. 25tl: EU/David Langfield. 25tr: Z/Damm. 26, 27t: Z. 27b: EU/Dorothy Burrows. 28: EU/JD. 29: Z/Damm. 30: Z/E. Carle.
Illustration on page 1 by Tom Powers.